Think for Yourself:

A Critical Thinking Workbook for Beginners

By: Dyreka Klaus

Table of Contents

Foreword

"It is the mark of an educated mind to be able to entertain a thought without accepting it," –
Aristotle

This quote from the famous Greek philosopher and scientist, captures the basis for the process of critical thinking. But what does it mean?

Aristotle knew that people are all too vulnerable to the influence of their own emotions. Often this can lead us to sloppy thinking patterns and behaviors. Emotions can sway us to reject ideas without even considering them! If we allow that, then we are missing out on knowledge and experiences. We miss out on gaining a better understanding of the people around us. We live only half of our lives, and that is a tragedy. Emotions have their place in our lives, but we need to be careful about when we use them, and to never let them use us.

What this quote best illustrates is that the skill of thinking about something – without allowing our own feelings to affect our thought process – is perhaps one of the most important that we can develop. By using the word "educated," Aristotle is telling people that they can learn how to do this. You do not have to be born with this ability.

By using the words "without accepting it" he is telling us that we have nothing to fear from ideas. Ideas cannot hurt you. They are only ideas. You have no reason to feel threatened or hurt by ideas. Ideas are separate from the imperfect people who believe them or use them for their own purposes. You might agree or disagree with someone on an idea, but for a totally different reason than they have. Ideas stand alone as a concept.

In the end, if you have considered an idea to the best of your ability, you may still disagree with it. You do not have to accept the idea as valid, or rational, or sensible. You may, at this point, file it away as something you don't agree with and pull it back out again later if you find new information about it. Nothing is forcing you to agree, so there is no harm in entertaining the thought. It is also important to note that there is nothing preventing you from changing your mind. It is yours and you may use it however you wish.

You might ask about the ways in which critical thinking can be used, and the answer is: in all ways. You can use critical thinking to determine what you feel to be morally right or morally wrong, but you can also use it to drive problem-solving and help yourself get through that math problem you're stuck on. You can use it to find a lost sock, or to repair a broken relationship.

Next, you might ask how one gets started. How can you learn to apply critical thinking? What, exactly, is the process for using it? These are the questions that this book is here to answer. it is a practical guide for learning and applying critical thinking skills. I hope that you find it useful for the rest of your life.

How to Use This Workbook

This workbook is divided into three sections: Basics, Practice, and Sources.

Basics: After each chapter or segment of a chapter that introduces a new concept, you will find a *Notes* section. This topic isn't one that is given to right and wrong answers, so your work will be to consider and research what you find here and record your thoughts, observations, tidbits from your research that you find helpful, URLs, and anything else you feel like you need to write down. This book isn't the alpha and omega of this topic. There is so much information that can easily be accessed on the internet, and your job will be to explore each concept to the best of your ability.

Practice: In this section of the workbook will be blank critical thinking steps pages. These are to help you practice working through problems that you come across in your daily life. When you have a problem to be solved or a question to be answered, or if you simply have a topic on your mind that you want to form an opinion on, you can open this book and use the practice pages to help you work through it.

Resources: As you look up information, practice good research skills by checking multiple sources. Chances are, you will come across at least one that can give you the "ah-ha!" moment you need. Even with definitions, it is important to understand that sources can still be biased so it is wise to check multiple sources. Doing this can give you a more coherent general idea of the concepts than one narrow view can. This section is where you can record good resources that you have found and may want to access again in the future.

What if I get stuck?

You may find that you have trouble understanding something in this workbook. Some of the concepts are complex, and some of the vocabulary isn't commonly used. When you run across anything you don't understand, I encourage you to ask someone else if they understand it and can help, or to look up more information on the topic or definitions for yourself. Mark, underline, dog-ear, and highlight this book at will. It is often useful to keep a reference in which we have been able to make our own notes or highlight what we do or don't understand.

We are fortunate to live in the information age. If you have internet access, then you have the entirety of human knowledge at your fingertips. You have news articles, research studies, education websites, YouTube, public domain literature, and so on. These days, even complete college coursework is available online for free. You also have access to many more people than previous generations had. Hit up social media and see what people have to say. Start conversations and consider different points of view. You can mine a huge cross section of humanity for information. Don't be afraid to seek it. You can teach yourself nearly anything you want to know with internet access and the ability to read. In short: Google it.

Basics

What is Critical Thinking (and Why Should I Care?)

Critical thinking – the objective analysis of an issue in order to form a judgment.

Problem solving – when you use critical thinking to overcome a difficulty.

Critical thinking is much like the *scientific process*. You will likely see many similarities and it may help to think of critical thinking as the scientific process that you can apply to things other than science. It is perhaps the most important skill you can develop after reading. In the same way that reading is the foundational skill for education, critical thinking is the foundational skill for development of your problem-solving skills. This spills over into every aspect of your life. New skills become easier to learn when you can think critically through obstacles. Problems seem more manageable when you can rationally analyze them for a solution. For these reasons, the ability to think critically is highly prized by employers. Learning this skill now, and practicing it regularly, will serve you well throughout your life.

Critical thinking is how you can arrive at a *reasonable answer*, or a *working theory*, when you are faced with a question or problem that does not have a readily apparent answer. This is done by being *objectively critical* of your own ideas or solutions and working to prove or disprove them to yourself. Initially, the process will feel laborious and even tedious, but over time – with practice – you will become very efficient at it and will be able to reason through most material problems within minutes. On the other hand, philosophical and metaphysical problems may never be answered to your complete satisfaction, and arguably this is a good thing. Philosophy is a fantastic way to practice critical thinking, and I encourage everyone with the reading level skills needed to study the works of the great philosophers to do so whenever the opportunity presents itself.

One of the core debates of metaphysics is the definition of truth. It is held by some that we are limited creatures and can never actually know the truth for sure. Fortunately, critical thinking isn't necessarily about finding the exact right answer every time. Rather, critical thinking is about *finding the best answer that you can find*, given the information that you have access to. Regular practice will hone your skill for this, and over time you will begin to arrive at judgments that not only make sense to you, but that are **logically consistent** with the available evidence. You will get better at asking relevant questions, and you will get better at forming theories for investigation. This skill is most useful in helping you form your best guess, or a premise that you can work from until you can gather more information. It is the way that you can break through the paralysis of indecision and start moving forward again.

One thing to remember is that the answer to your problem wasn't obvious, and that there may be no one true answer. Critical thinking is often used to form personal opinions, so don't make the mistake of thinking that the answer you arrived at must be true for everyone else. In some cases, you may find an objectively true answer that fits the evidence with a 100%

replicable result, but in the vast majority of cases that will not happen, and you will only find a personal theory regarding the answer.

It is crucial to revisit your conclusions whenever you are presented with new evidence or ideas that challenge them. Never think that you have it all figured out and can dismiss new information off hand. **There is always a chance that you were wrong**. The most useful thing we can do is to keep from getting emotionally attached to our conclusions. If you were wrong about something, it serves no purpose to become angry, hurt, or vengeful over it. That is a waste of energy and focus. It does nothing to make the situation better and is likely to make it much worse. It is better for our relationships with others and even for our own health to be able to calmly consider new information, accept that we were wrong, and agree to consider new possibilities. There is no shame in doing this, or even in asking for some time to consider the new evidence and possibilities. This displays a steady maturity to others that draws respect, even from those who may dislike us. Life is much easier when you have earned the respect of those around you.

None of this is to say that emotion doesn't have its rightful place in our lives, because it most certainly does. It even has its place in this process. The pivotal concept here though is that we must be able to remove emotion when it is getting in our way, and add it when we need it, with the understanding that it is *not logic*, and that it can only complete an opinion, not facts. Sometimes we hit the limit of our ability to apply logic and evidence without arriving at a solid answer. At these times, we can then filter the possibilities through our own emotions if we remain aware of the point at which our process switched from evidentiary to emotional. This is the point at which we have completed critical thinking for the time being. We can form an opinion, rather than leave the question unanswered. At times, we may need to do this to make a decision. If there is no decision riding on the answer, then we are at liberty to leave the question open until a later date if we wish, and don't have to rely on our emotions or instincts for the final choice.

Notes:

_Critical thinking is not about ___, an idea is an idea, but those who ___ ___ ___ good ideas. Think for yourself_

_____

_____

_____

_____

_____

_____

_____

_____

_____

_____

_____

_____

_____

The Types of Reasoning

"I have not failed. I've just found 10,000 ways that won't work." - Thomas A. Edison

When employing critical thinking or the scientific method to a given problem, there are three main types of reasoning that may be used to draw conclusions: **deductive**, **inductive**, and **abductive**. All three types of reasoning are useful in their own right and can be especially effective when used together. The style of critical thinking laid out in this workbook may use all three methods when and where appropriate, as decided by the thinker (you).

Deductive Reasoning (based on theory):

Deductive reasoning, or "deduction," begins with a basic thought, statement, or hypothesis and then analyzes the possibilities to reach a conclusion. It is a valid form of logical reasoning and will be the basis for the steps of critical thinking laid out in this workbook.

Deductive reasoning is used to test theories. First, we would form our basic theory or hypothesis. Next, we would form a prediction of the results of our theory. After that, we would gather data regarding the subject. Finally, we would analyze our prediction to determine if it fits the data or if we're working with a faulty premise. When used scientifically, this often lends itself to experimentation and results. When used in critical thinking, it can do the same or it can be used backward to deduce likely explanations or past conditions for a current problem.

Deduction relies on the premises – or original information – being correct. If one of your premises isn't true, you can arrive at a conclusion that is logical given the premises but that is not actually true. This is a valuable tool for eliminating premises that are faulty. With deductive reasoning, we start with a general idea and make it more specific. We predict what the result *should* be *if* the premise is correct.

For example, from the premise that all humans can die, and the premise that John is a human, we can *deduce* that John can die. This is logical and correct to the best of human knowledge and experience. On the other hand, if we begin with the premise that all grandfathers have grey hair, and the premise that John is a grandfather, we may deduce logically that John has grey hair. This is logical according to the premises we were working with, but it is not necessarily true since our first premise was not true. When we investigate, we may find that John has brown hair, or even that he is bald. In this way, we were able to eliminate a faulty premise and narrow down our hypotheses to those most likely to be true.

Notes:

_____

_____

_____

_____

<u>Important Concepts</u>

There are some foundational concepts that should be understood if you are going to be exploring and using critical thinking skills. You can't build a house without a foundation. If you were to try, you would end up with a crooked house that could easily be knocked down. Likewise, you can't build this skill without these concepts. If you try, you will end up with poorly reasoned ideas that can easily be disproven.

The concepts are:

- <u>Objective vs. Subjective</u> –

  - An **objective** observation is one that relies on what is provable with evidence. Objective observations, or **facts**, can be proven true by anyone who cares to investigate them. The results of investigation are reliably repeatable. Example: *All apples are fruit.*

  - A **subjective** observation is one that relies on what is felt emotionally. Subjective observations, or **opinions**, are dependent on the experiences and interpretations of the individual. The results of investigation will depend on who is doing the investigating. Example: *Honeycrisp apples taste the best.*

Notes:

_____
_____
_____
_____
_____
_____

- <u>Definitions</u> – It is crucially important that we consider things as exactly what they are and not what we hope they are, or even what most people think they are. A thing can only be exactly what it is and applying extra layers of meaning as if they were facts will only muddy the thought waters. It will prevent you from taking in new information.

Example: A flower. We know what its individual parts are (stem, leaf, petal, stamen, etc.). We know or can find the scientific chemical composition. We know or can find the scientific name. We know that it is a plant and will grow in the right conditions. What we cannot know is that it is beautiful or that it smells sweet. We cannot know all the common usage names that it has been given, and we cannot know how much another individual may value it. We cannot know these things because they are subjective. So, the claim "Morning Glories are beautiful," is not true. Not everyone will agree with you, and some may even call it by a different name. The claim "I find Morning Glories to be beautiful," is a more accurate statement.

Notes:

_____
_____
_____
_____
_____

- <u>Internal vs. External</u> –

  o An **internal** concept is one that happens within the mind of the individual

  o An **external** concept is one that is imposed on the individual by someone else

Example: The concept of "cooperation" is an internal concept. It is a choice made by the individual, inside their own mind. On the other hand, "coercion" is an external concept, since it is the act of making or forcing someone to do something. Both cooperation and coercion may (or may not) produce similar results, but they arrived at the results very differently and this is an important distinction to recognize.

Notes:

_____
_____
_____
_____
_____

- <u>There Is Always Room for Improvement</u> – None of us are perfect. We all have our own strengths and weaknesses. The person who is disagreeing with you has their own room for improvement, just as you do. It is important to understand that your understanding may never be perfect. If something or someone challenges your understanding, it is not an attack. It does not mean that you, or they, are stupid. It doesn't mean that you didn't do your best in the past, and it doesn't mean that you can't do your best in the future. An important additional concept is that even people who you trust, or feel that you should be able to trust, can still make mistakes and may not have all the answers.

Notes:

_____
_____
_____
_____
_____
_____

- Intellectual Honesty – Intellectual honesty is your ability to accept the conclusions of your own investigation, whether it is what you were hoping it would be or not. Just because someone you like says that something is true does not mean that it is, in fact, true. Likewise, just because someone you *dislike* says that something is true does not mean that it is *untrue*. If it is important to you, you should always be willing to fully investigate it for yourself, without emotional **bias**, and with a willingness to accept the idea that you may have been wrong. Example: *"I don't have to try them to know that I don't like Brussels Sprouts,"* is intellectually dishonest. You cannot rationally form an opinion on a taste that you have never experienced. *"I won't like them because my twin brother does not like them,"* is also intellectually dishonest. The statement, *"I have no wish to try Brussels Sprouts,"* is intellectually honest. You are being honest about your feelings without shifting blame or making excuses.

Notes:

_____

_____

_____

_____

_____

_____

- Positive Claims vs. Negative Claims –

  - A **positive claim** is based on the idea of *yes*, or something that is present and verifiable.

  - A **negative claim** is based on the idea of *no*, or the absence of something.

Example: "Yes, I have a widget," is a positive claim. You can prove that you have a widget by simply producing said widget. "No, I do not have a widget," is a negative claim. You are making a claim about the absence of something. This cannot be proven, because you can't produce *nothing* as your evidence. Some negative claims can be proven at least to the satisfaction of the listener, often by process of elimination, but in general it is impossible to prove most negative claims.

One example of a negative claim that cannot be proven is when someone claims, *"there is no way to do that."* Logically speaking, they are unable to prove this claim. That does not mean that the opposite positive claim - *"there must be a way to do that,"* - is true by default. Each claim must be proven with evidence; just remember that negative claims are highly unlikely to have any available evidence. The exceptions to this generality would be claims like "I don't have any Irish ancestry." The claim is a negative claim, but it can be proven or disproven with a DNA test. In fact, the claim could be reworded as a positive claim and still carry the same meaning, such as "I only have Swedish and French ancestry." Often these provable negative claims are simply misstated positive claims.

In philosophical circles, it is widely thought that this puts the **burden of proof** on the person making the **positive claim**. If I were to claim that you have my bike, I would need to prove that by showing that my bike is in your possession if I wanted my claim to be accepted as the truth. You can claim that you do not have my bike until you're blue in the face, but you can't present the absence of my bike in your possession as evidence to a 100% certainty.

Notes:

_____

_____

_____

_____

_____

- <u>Occam's Razor</u> – Occam's Razor is a problem-solving principle attributed to Franciscan friar, William of Occam (c 1287-1347AD). The principle states that **among competing hypotheses, the one with the fewest assumptions should be selected**. In other words, the hypothesis that relies the least on guessing or assuming things is the one most likely to be logically sound. Another way to express this idea is: the simplest explanation is the most likely to be correct.

Notes:

_____

_____

_____

_____

_____

_____

First Principles

First Principles Thinking – or **Reasoning by First Principles** – is breaking ideas down to their most basic elements for complete examination. In essence, it is the act of reverse-engineering complex concepts until you have the building blocks those concepts are built from, then analyzing each piece for validity before reassembling the valid pieces and possibly new pieces as well. This was a favorite approach of Aristotle and has been successfully employed by many of the world's great thinkers and innovators. A notable modern example is Elon Musk.

A First Principle is a basic concept, idea, or fact that stands alone and cannot be said to rest on any other concepts, ideas, or facts. If ideas were math problems, the First Principles would be number concepts, such as "1 means one of something, 2 means two of something, etc." These concepts simply are, and we cannot arrive at them from any other facts or concepts. They stand alone as the very foundation of the topic.

When we break a problem or question down into First Principles, we are better able to avoid the murkiness of faulty assumptions and reasoning. We are then not taking anything on faith and are instead building our own understanding of the problem or topic independent of any biased influences. Aristotle called First Principles, "the first basis from which a thing is known."

As mental models go, First Principles is perhaps the most indispensable toward improving your critical thinking skills. It is a core piece of the creative process. There is a huge difference between originality and copies. Creative artists rethink the process from the very bottom and create something new. Innovators do the same. Critical thinkers must strive to emulate the creative/innovative process by *letting go of what they think they know and beginning at the beginning*.

A good example that highlights the difference between creation and copy and embodies the concept of First Principles is the distinction between a *cook* and a *chef*. A cook is someone who follows recipes while a chef is someone who creates new recipes. A chef knows and understands flavor and texture profiles as well as how they interact with each other. A chef uses the basic knowledge of flavors to create new combinations of flavors. A chef has broken food down into its most basic elements and become familiar with them, then reimagined the ways they can be put together to create food.

Now let's examine an example of First Principles in critical thinking. Let's say that a young girl is trying to figure out what she wants to do with her life. Some people tell her that her place is to stay home and raise children, others tell her that she owes it to womankind to climb the corporate ladder and break glass ceilings. Her mother has made it clear that her feelings will be hurt if the girl chooses anything other than following in her footsteps to be a school teacher. Her father believes that she needs a husband to take care of her. Her friends want her to travel the world for a few years with them before she decides on anything. And her boyfriend wants her to go to the same college he's going to.

The girl has become paralyzed by indecision due to all the conflicting wants, pressures, and expectations that have been placed on her by others. She decides to look at her problem by reasoning through first principles. She thinks about it and managed to boil the situation down to a few base concepts. The first is that it is her life and nobody else's. Whatever choice she makes, she is the one who will have to live with the results. She also deduces that none of these other people have a right to expect anything from her. And finally, she concludes that only she can truly know herself, what her strengths and weaknesses are, where her passions lie, and what her hopes and dreams for the future are. These are all first principles. Her life, her choice, only she can know what is right for her.

Realizing this enables her to cut out all of the extra noise and confusion and focus on deciding what she really wants out of life. She considers all of her options and chooses to pursue an archaeology degree at a school that is not the same one her boyfriend is going to. She was empowered to find a path that wasn't on anyone else's radar for her, but that was the most likely to lead to her own success in meeting her goals.

For another example, imagine that an inventor wanted to build a better mousetrap. Nobody likes dealing with mousetraps. They're dangerous, gory, inhumane, and a big hassle. There had to be a way to improve on their design, right? After researching all previous attempts by people to solve the problem, the inventor wasn't so sure that the mousetrap design could be effectively improved on, so he broke the problem down into first principles. He ended up realizing that people want a way to rid their homes and farms of mice, but it doesn't necessarily have to be a *trap*. There may be another way to keep rodents out of homes and harvests. Because of this realization that he arrived at through first principles, he was then able to research mice and their behavior. He did his homework on their physiology and ended up inventing a sonic rodent deterrent that could be plugged into an outlet and would drive mice (and other such pests) away with no further mess or bother for the homeowner. He turned an entire industry on its head, provided a better solution for consumers, and made a comfortable living, all because he was able to deconstruct the problem back to a point where something completely new could be done. This is often referred to as "thinking outside the box".

When we employ First Principles, we are not taking anything on faith except the most fundamental concepts that cannot be any further reduced than they already are. We strip away all the assumptions, all the things people think they know about a topic, all the traditional solutions, until what we are left with is wide open possibility and an opportunity for a new way. This can be extremely useful when applied to problems that feel insurmountable.

Notes:

_____

_____

_____

_____

_____

_____

Logical Fallacies

In practice, critical thinking is a lot like having a debate with yourself. You have a theory, or claim, and it is your responsibility to try to either prove/disprove it to yourself or rationalize/reject it. Because of this, some of the standard rules for logical debate are very useful tools. The most relevant of these is the ability to recognize logical fallacies.

A **fallacy** is an untruth, or something presented as a fact, which cannot be proven to be a fact. If you can learn to recognize when something is not necessarily true, and why it is not necessarily true, then you will have a much more successful investigation. A **logical fallacy** is a mistake in logical thinking. It is important to remember that spotting a logical fallacy *doesn't prove the premise false*. It only shows you that the *argument* that you are using is not a sound argument. We must be able to separate sound arguments from those that are not sound. If you can eliminate the fallacious arguments, you will be more able to explore the sound arguments.

Without further ado, let's jump into a list of the most commonly used logical fallacies, what they mean, and why they invalidate an argument.

- Ad Hominem – This is probably the most commonly used logical fallacy, and also the easiest to spot. An Ad Hominem fallacy is when one person will use a personal opinion about another as justification for rejecting their claim.

Example: *"You have a silly haircut, so you must be silly, which makes everything you say silly, which makes this argument of yours silly."*

This is not a logical conclusion for this person to draw from the available evidence. When someone uses an Ad Hominem fallacy, they are focusing on their opponent and not on the evidence.

The character or appearance of the other person has absolutely nothing to do with the evidence that they have presented. Evidence must be considered alone for what it is, and for the information it may or may not provide.

- Appeal to Popularity – The Appeal to Popularity fallacy is when you point to how many people like or agree with a thing or idea as proof that it is correct, or right, or good.

Example: *"Everyone at school likes Jim, so that must mean he's a good guy."*

This is a fallacy. Popular opinion can be and often is wrong. Maybe Jim is a bully, and everyone is pretending to like him because they are afraid of him. Or maybe Jim is a very good liar, so everyone that likes him doesn't know the truth about what kind of person he is. Or possibly Jim really is a great and trustworthy guy. You can't know for sure which is true. Just because many people agree on something does not necessarily make them right. Agreement and popularity are not facts or evidence. Popularity is not truth, because if popular opinion changes then the truth would change with it and the truth does not change. The truth is always the truth.

- Appeal to Tradition – The Appeal to Tradition fallacy is when you claim that something is right, or true, or must be done one way simply because it has always been seen as right, has always been viewed as true, or has always been done that way.

Example: *"We have always baked cookies on Sundays, so we can't bake cookies on Wednesday."*

Just because an idea or practice is old, does not mean that it is right or is the only way. You assuredly can bake cookies on Wednesday, if you wish to. Whether you would have to rearrange the rest of your schedule to make that work out *well* is irrelevant to the truth of whether or not you are capable of baking cookies on Wednesday.

- Appeal to Novelty – The Appeal to Novelty fallacy is the opposite of the Appeal to Tradition. The Appeal to Novelty states that something must be right, or good, or true simply because it is new. This is usually based on a prior rejection of the traditional thought, idea, or process.

Example: *"Scientists have a new theory about cancer treatment, so it must be the best since it is the latest thing."*

This is a fallacy because the only evidence being considered is how new the information is. The claim presumes that the newest thing is the best thing. This is not always true. Sometimes new things are better, and sometimes they are not. Sometimes they are even very much like existing things. How old or new the information, thing, or theory is, has nothing to do with how good or right it is.

- Appeal to Emotion – An Appeal to Emotion is when you try to get agreement from others by making them feel a certain emotion. This could be anger, or pity, or empathy, or happiness, or sadness, etc.

Example: *"You have to do it because I was really looking forward to it."*

This argument is appealing to the emotion sympathy. If you use this argument, then you are telling the other person they *have to* do what you want because they should feel sorry for you. This is untrue. They do not have to do anything. They don't even have to feel sorry for you. Your expectations are not their responsibility, they are yours. Manipulating the emotions of others is not – and has no relationship to – evidence or reason, and so it is a failure in logic.

- <u>Appeal to Authority</u> – The Appeal to Authority fallacy is when you insist that your claim is true because an alleged authority figure agrees with you.

Example: *"Tesla's experiments were dangerous and useless because Thomas Edison said so."*

In this case, you have established someone as a purported authority on the topic at hand (Edison) and used his opinions of his competitor (Tesla) as evidence that the competitor's work was dangerous and useless. You are not providing evidence, just an opinion from someone else. You are not discussing the work, or even Tesla's own opinions about it as the origin source, but again are using the opinions of a third party. You are expecting your opponent to accept on faith that Edison was indeed an expert and that he wasn't mistaken or lying, and you are asking them to suspend their awareness of how the claim is based on subjective evaluations to begin with. When you Appeal to Authority, you are offering only second-hand opinions as evidence. You haven't even proven that Edison did, in fact, say that. Faith is not evidence. "Just believe me because this other person said so," is a fallacious argument.

- <u>Red Herring</u> – A Red Herring fallacy is when you try to distract away from the topic at hand by bringing up irrelevant ideas or points.

Example: *"I know you think a puppy is too much work, but just look at how cute they are."*

The appearance of the puppy has no relevance on how much work it is to care for one. The topic at hand is the care of puppies, and using this tactic is fallacious because you are refusing to even talk about the real topic. You're changing the subject. This is not an argument but is rather more of an avoidance of the other person's argument.

- <u>Arguing from Ignorance</u> – The Arguing from Ignorance fallacy is when you argue that something is true because it is not known to be false.

Example: *"Bigfoot must exist because nobody has been able to debunk the footprint molds"*

Just because nobody has been able to disprove something does not automatically make it true. All it means is that it has not yet been proven or disproven. Lack of a better answer does not necessarily make your answer the right one.

- <u>Begging the Question</u> – Begging the Question is also known as *circular reasoning*. This happens when you use your own claim, or parts of it, as evidence to support your claim.

Example: *"I have a right to be healthy, so you have to give me this medicine because I need it to be healthy."*

The claim cannot even be argued against because agreement is already assumed in the **premise**, or the original evidence presented. This type of argument fails as proof because only someone who accepts the original premise will be able to accept the conclusion. I would have to agree that your premise "I have a right..." is correct in order to be persuaded to accept that I am wrong if I do not do as you say.

- <u>Straw Man</u> – The Straw Man fallacy is when you misrepresent an argument or evidence to make it seem weaker, disprove your version of it, then conclude that you have disproven the argument or evidence.

Example:

Person A: *"Romeo was in love with Juliette."*

Person B: *"So you're saying that he wanted to die with her? That's just not true, because he didn't want to die at all according to what he said at this point in the play."*

The only thing Person B has argued against is the notion that Romeo wanted to die with Juliette. He hasn't managed to disprove or even address the matter of Romeo's romantic feelings for Juliette, which were presented as a stand-alone statement or claim and did not address anything else. Person B has concluded that Person A is wrong by arguing against something that Person A never even said to begin with.

- <u>Sweeping Generalizations and Hasty Generalizations</u> –

  - The Sweeping Generalizations Fallacy is when you take something that is true a lot of the time and use it as evidence that it must be true this time.
  - The Hasty Generalization fallacy is when you conclude that something is true this time, so it must be true every time.

These fallacies often mirror each other. The concept can typically be stated either way.

Example:

"Boys love video games, so my boyfriend will love it if I get him one for his birthday." This is a sweeping generalization.

"My brother loves video games, so my boyfriend must, since they're both boys." This is a hasty generalization.

You can see how the two types of generalization fallacies can feed on each other. In this case, if you go through it backward, a hasty generalization was used to form a sweeping generalization, and this was ultimately used to make a decision without any actual knowledge of the boyfriend's likes and dislikes.

- <u>No True Scotsman</u> – The No True Scotsman Fallacy is when you dismiss evidence that doesn't support your claim by saying that the evidence is not authentic or relevant. The best example for this fallacy is the example that it is named after.

Example:

Person A: "No Scotsman puts sugar on their porridge."

Person B: "Angus over in Edinburgh does."

Person A: "Then Angus is no true Scotsman."

Person A is using their own premise as the reason that they are dismissing the evidence. They are claiming that their original statement that Scotsmen do not put sugar on their porridge still stands, because Angus doesn't meet their own standard for what a Scotsman is (namely, one who does not put sugar on their porridge). They are playing with definitions to support their own claim. This is not a sound argument. Edinburgh is in Scotland. Angus is a Scottish name. It is likely that Angus is, in fact, a Scotsman. Person A is dismissing all of this other evidence in favor of imposing their own interpretation of the definition of a Scotsman.

Notes:

_____
_____
_____
_____
_____
_____
_____
_____
_____
_____
_____
_____
_____
_____
_____
_____
_____
_____
_____
_____

The Steps of Critical Thinking

When you want to use critical thinking, there are some steps that you can follow in order to keep your thought process organized. These steps are broadly based on deductive reasoning, but within each step you can apply all three types of reasoning according to the needs of the problem. Some people run through these steps instinctively, and perhaps out of order, without even realizing what they're doing. Others may need to be shown the process. Even a person with a knack for critical thinking can benefit from unpacking and studying the steps they're unconsciously using. So, what are the steps?

STEP 1: Develop Your Understanding of the Problem or Claim

Typically, a good place to start is to ask questions. Who, what, when, where, why, and how are questions that you can ask to establish which facts you have and which facts you're missing. "I don't know," is an acceptable answer to any of these. It just indicates that you have some investigation to do. It is possible and even likely that one or more of these questions will not be relevant to your problem. Answering the ones that you can is still important for developing your understanding of exactly what the problem is, and what type of information you'll need to solve it. Be very careful to reserve judgment at this point. You don't want to introduce any pre-conceived notions right now if you can help it. This is the best place to apply First Principles.

STEP 2: Develop a Hypothesis

This is where you get to use your imagination. Give yourself free reign to imagine possible truth scenarios, ideas, or solutions. Use the facts that you established in Step 1 to build ideas that fit with those facts. It is important at this point to examine your own motivations and biases. You should be asking yourself if you're hoping for a certain outcome, or if you're leaning one way or the other regarding which hypothesis you will work with. We all have our biases and pre-conceived notions, but it is important that we examine them and take note of their presence. This can help us guard against allowing them to falsely manipulate our results.

STEP 3: Investigate (gather data)

In this step, you will investigate, research, and examine information about your hypothesis. Consider all possible sources as worthy of investigation. A source can be anything or anyone that can provide information. People can be sources, books can be sources, the internet can be a source, observation can be a source, and experimentation can be a source. Remember that you are gathering *information*, not necessarily *truth*. Sources can be biased or wrong. This step is simply about gathering what sources have to offer and categorizing it based on applicability and reliability.

For example, you may find a news article supporting one of your hypotheses but also find a medical paper written by a subject matter expert that supports the opposite position. You will consider both source materials *and* take into account the credentials, professional standing, likely motivations, incentives, and possible biases of the two authors. The journalist may be incentivized to sell papers by twisting facts to produce something shocking. On the other hand, a research scientist may be funded by a company with a financial interest in suppressing the facts to protect their market shares, so the scientist may feel pressured to lie in order to keep their job. In the end, all sources are rooted in humanity, which is imperfect. Consider what they provide carefully but stay skeptical and investigate thoroughly.

STEP 4: Analyze Your Results

In this step, you will challenge your own ideas with the data you gathered. You will be trying to look at your ideas from all different angles and seeing if the observations fit with your theory. If they do not fit with your theory, then you may conclude that your theory was wrong. If the data does fit with your theory, you may conclude that your theory is correct or only conclude that your theory is *likely*. After all, in many cases you cannot ever know for sure that you have all the data. However, for most applications a likely theory is sufficient, especially if you remain aware that it is still a theory.

STEP 5: Apply Personal Preferences (if appropriate)

This step is optional and only applicable to certain types of problems. This is where you can allow emotional consideration. Some problems will have no logical conclusion or will not have a conclusion that is sufficiently logical to outweigh your personal feelings on the matter. In these cases, you will make an emotional decision in the end. This is a perfectly acceptable way to make many decisions, but don't forget to be intellectually honest about when your decision was emotional.

Notes:

_____
_____
_____
_____
_____
_____
_____
_____
_____
_____
_____
_____

Practice

PROBLEM:

_____
_____
_____

STEP 1: Develop Your Understanding of the Problem

_____
_____
_____
_____
_____
_____
_____
_____
_____
_____
_____
_____
_____
_____

STEP 2: Develop a Hypothesis

_____
_____
_____
_____
_____
_____

STEP 3: Investigate/Gather Data (record sources if possible)

_____
_____
_____
_____
_____
_____
_____
_____
_____
_____

STEP 4: Analyze Your Results

_____
_____
_____
_____
_____
_____
_____
_____
_____
_____
_____
_____
_____
_____
_____
_____
_____
_____

STEP 5: Apply Personal Preference (optional)

_____
_____
_____
_____
_____
_____

CONCLUSION:

_____
_____
_____
_____
_____
_____
_____
_____
_____
_____

PROBLEM:

_____
_____
_____

STEP 1: Develop Your Understanding of the Problem

_____
_____
_____
_____
_____
_____
_____
_____
_____
_____
_____
_____
_____
_____

STEP 2: Develop a Hypothesis

_____
_____
_____
_____
_____
_____

STEP 3: Investigate/Gather Data (record sources if possible)

_____
_____
_____
_____
_____
_____
_____
_____
_____
_____

STEP 4: Analyze Your Results

_____
_____
_____
_____
_____
_____
_____
_____
_____
_____
_____
_____
_____
_____
_____
_____
_____
_____
_____
_____

STEP 5: Apply Personal Preference (optional)

_____
_____
_____
_____
_____
_____

CONCLUSION:

_____
_____
_____
_____
_____
_____
_____
_____
_____
_____
_____

PROBLEM:

_____
_____
_____

STEP 1: Develop Your Understanding of the Problem

_____
_____
_____
_____
_____
_____
_____
_____
_____
_____
_____
_____
_____
_____

STEP 2: Develop a Hypothesis

_____
_____
_____
_____
_____
_____

STEP 3: Investigate/Gather Data (record sources if possible)

_____
_____
_____
_____
_____
_____
_____
_____
_____
_____
_____

STEP 4: Analyze Your Results

_____
_____
_____
_____
_____
_____
_____
_____
_____
_____
_____
_____
_____
_____
_____
_____
_____
_____

STEP 5: Apply Personal Preference (optional)

_____
_____
_____
_____
_____
_____

CONCLUSION:

_____
_____
_____
_____
_____
_____
_____
_____
_____
_____
_____

PROBLEM:

_____

_____

_____

STEP 1: Develop Your Understanding of the Problem

_____

_____

_____

_____

_____

_____

_____

_____

_____

_____

_____

_____

_____

_____

STEP 2: Develop a Hypothesis

_____

_____

_____

_____

_____

_____

STEP 3: Investigate/Gather Data (record sources if possible)

_____

_____

_____

_____

_____

_____

_____

_____

_____

_____

STEP 4: Analyze Your Results

_____
_____
_____
_____
_____
_____
_____
_____
_____
_____
_____
_____
_____
_____
_____
_____
_____
_____
_____
_____

STEP 5: Apply Personal Preference (optional)

_____
_____
_____
_____
_____
_____

CONCLUSION:

_____
_____
_____
_____
_____
_____
_____
_____
_____
_____

PROBLEM:

_____
_____
_____

STEP 1: Develop Your Understanding of the Problem

_____
_____
_____
_____
_____
_____
_____
_____
_____
_____
_____
_____
_____

STEP 2: Develop a Hypothesis

_____
_____
_____
_____
_____
_____

STEP 3: Investigate/Gather Data (record sources if possible)

_____
_____
_____
_____
_____
_____
_____
_____
_____
_____

STEP 4: Analyze Your Results

_____
_____
_____
_____
_____
_____
_____
_____
_____
_____
_____
_____
_____
_____
_____
_____
_____

STEP 5: Apply Personal Preference (optional)

_____
_____
_____
_____
_____
_____

CONCLUSION:

_____
_____
_____
_____
_____
_____
_____
_____
_____
_____
_____

PROBLEM:

_____
_____
_____

STEP 1: Develop Your Understanding of the Problem

_____
_____
_____
_____
_____
_____
_____
_____
_____
_____
_____
_____
_____
_____
_____

STEP 2: Develop a Hypothesis

_____
_____
_____
_____
_____
_____

STEP 3: Investigate/Gather Data (record sources if possible)

_____
_____
_____
_____
_____
_____
_____
_____
_____

STEP 4: Analyze Your Results

_____
_____
_____
_____
_____
_____
_____
_____
_____
_____
_____
_____
_____
_____
_____
_____
_____
_____
_____

STEP 5: Apply Personal Preference (optional)

_____
_____
_____
_____
_____
_____

CONCLUSION:

_____
_____
_____
_____
_____
_____
_____
_____
_____
_____
_____

PROBLEM:

_____
_____
_____

STEP 1: Develop Your Understanding of the Problem

_____
_____
_____
_____
_____
_____
_____
_____
_____
_____
_____
_____
_____
_____

STEP 2: Develop a Hypothesis

_____
_____
_____
_____
_____
_____

STEP 3: Investigate/Gather Data (record sources if possible)

_____
_____
_____
_____
_____
_____
_____
_____
_____
_____

STEP 4: Analyze Your Results

_____

_____

_____

_____

_____

_____

_____

_____

_____

_____

_____

_____

_____

_____

_____

_____

_____

_____

_____

STEP 5: Apply Personal Preference (optional)

_____

_____

_____

_____

_____

_____

CONCLUSION:

_____

_____

_____

_____

_____

_____

_____

_____

_____

_____

_____

PROBLEM:

_____

_____

_____

STEP 1: Develop Your Understanding of the Problem

_____

_____

_____

_____

_____

_____

_____

_____

_____

_____

_____

_____

_____

STEP 2: Develop a Hypothesis

_____

_____

_____

_____

_____

STEP 3: Investigate/Gather Data (record sources if possible)

_____

_____

_____

_____

_____

_____

_____

_____

_____

STEP 4: Analyze Your Results

_____
_____
_____
_____
_____
_____
_____
_____
_____
_____
_____
_____
_____
_____
_____
_____
_____
_____
_____

STEP 5: Apply Personal Preference (optional)

_____
_____
_____
_____
_____
_____

CONCLUSION:

_____
_____
_____
_____
_____
_____
_____
_____
_____
_____

PROBLEM:

_____
_____
_____

STEP 1: Develop Your Understanding of the Problem

_____
_____
_____
_____
_____
_____
_____
_____
_____
_____
_____
_____
_____
_____

STEP 2: Develop a Hypothesis

_____
_____
_____
_____
_____
_____

STEP 3: Investigate/Gather Data (record sources if possible)

_____
_____
_____
_____
_____
_____
_____
_____
_____
_____

STEP 4: Analyze Your Results

_____
_____
_____
_____
_____
_____
_____
_____
_____
_____
_____
_____
_____
_____
_____

STEP 5: Apply Personal Preference (optional)

_____
_____
_____
_____
_____
_____

CONCLUSION:

_____
_____
_____
_____
_____
_____
_____
_____
_____

PROBLEM:

_____
_____
_____

STEP 1: Develop Your Understanding of the Problem

_____
_____
_____
_____
_____
_____
_____
_____
_____
_____
_____
_____
_____
_____

STEP 2: Develop a Hypothesis

_____
_____
_____
_____
_____
_____

STEP 3: Investigate/Gather Data (record sources if possible)

_____
_____
_____
_____
_____
_____
_____
_____
_____
_____

STEP 4: Analyze Your Results

_____

_____

_____

_____

_____

_____

_____

_____

_____

_____

_____

_____

_____

_____

_____

_____

_____

_____

STEP 5: Apply Personal Preference (optional)

_____

_____

_____

_____

_____

_____

CONCLUSION:

_____

_____

_____

_____

_____

_____

_____

_____

_____

_____

PROBLEM:

_____

_____

_____

STEP 1: Develop Your Understanding of the Problem

_____

_____

_____

_____

_____

_____

_____

_____

_____

_____

_____

_____

_____

STEP 2: Develop a Hypothesis

_____

_____

_____

_____

_____

_____

STEP 3: Investigate/Gather Data (record sources if possible)

_____

_____

_____

_____

_____

_____

_____

_____

_____

_____

STEP 4: Analyze Your Results

_____
_____
_____
_____
_____
_____
_____
_____
_____
_____
_____
_____
_____
_____
_____
_____
_____
_____

STEP 5: Apply Personal Preference (optional)

_____
_____
_____
_____
_____
_____

CONCLUSION:

_____
_____
_____
_____
_____
_____
_____
_____
_____
_____

PROBLEM:

_____
_____
_____

STEP 1: Develop Your Understanding of the Problem

_____
_____
_____
_____
_____
_____
_____
_____
_____
_____
_____
_____
_____
_____

STEP 2: Develop a Hypothesis

_____
_____
_____
_____
_____
_____

STEP 3: Investigate/Gather Data (record sources if possible)

_____
_____
_____
_____
_____
_____
_____
_____
_____
_____

STEP 4: Analyze Your Results

_____
_____
_____
_____
_____
_____
_____
_____
_____
_____
_____
_____
_____
_____
_____
_____
_____

STEP 5: Apply Personal Preference (optional)

_____
_____
_____
_____
_____
_____

CONCLUSION:

_____
_____
_____
_____
_____
_____
_____
_____
_____
_____

PROBLEM:

_____

_____

_____

STEP 1: Develop Your Understanding of the Problem

_____

_____

_____

_____

_____

_____

_____

_____

_____

_____

_____

_____

_____

_____

_____

STEP 2: Develop a Hypothesis

_____

_____

_____

_____

_____

_____

STEP 3: Investigate/Gather Data (record sources if possible)

_____

_____

_____

_____

_____

_____

_____

_____

_____

_____

_____

STEP 4: Analyze Your Results

_____
_____
_____
_____
_____
_____
_____
_____
_____
_____
_____
_____
_____
_____
_____
_____
_____
_____

STEP 5: Apply Personal Preference (optional)

_____
_____
_____
_____
_____
_____

CONCLUSION:

_____
_____
_____
_____
_____
_____
_____
_____
_____
_____

PROBLEM:

_____

_____

_____

STEP 1: Develop Your Understanding of the Problem

_____

_____

_____

_____

_____

_____

_____

_____

_____

_____

_____

_____

_____

_____

STEP 2: Develop a Hypothesis

_____

_____

_____

_____

_____

_____

STEP 3: Investigate/Gather Data (record sources if possible)

_____

_____

_____

_____

_____

_____

_____

_____

_____

STEP 4: Analyze Your Results

_____
_____
_____
_____
_____
_____
_____
_____
_____
_____
_____
_____
_____
_____
_____
_____
_____
_____
_____
_____

STEP 5: Apply Personal Preference (optional)

_____
_____
_____
_____
_____
_____

CONCLUSION:

_____
_____
_____
_____
_____
_____
_____
_____
_____
_____
_____

PROBLEM:

_____
_____
_____

STEP 1: Develop Your Understanding of the Problem

_____
_____
_____
_____
_____
_____
_____
_____
_____
_____
_____
_____
_____
_____

STEP 2: Develop a Hypothesis

_____
_____
_____
_____
_____
_____

STEP 3: Investigate/Gather Data (record sources if possible)

_____
_____
_____
_____
_____
_____
_____
_____
_____
_____

STEP 4: Analyze Your Results

_____
_____
_____
_____
_____
_____
_____
_____
_____
_____
_____
_____
_____
_____
_____
_____
_____
_____
_____

STEP 5: Apply Personal Preference (optional)

_____
_____
_____
_____
_____
_____

CONCLUSION:

_____
_____
_____
_____
_____
_____
_____
_____
_____
_____
_____
_____

PROBLEM:

_____

_____

_____

STEP 1: Develop Your Understanding of the Problem

_____

_____

_____

_____

_____

_____

_____

_____

_____

_____

_____

_____

_____

_____

_____

STEP 2: Develop a Hypothesis

_____

_____

_____

_____

_____

STEP 3: Investigate/Gather Data (record sources if possible)

_____

_____

_____

_____

_____

_____

_____

_____

_____

_____

STEP 4: Analyze Your Results

_____
_____
_____
_____
_____
_____
_____
_____
_____
_____
_____
_____
_____
_____
_____
_____
_____
_____

STEP 5: Apply Personal Preference (optional)

_____
_____
_____
_____
_____
_____

CONCLUSION:

_____
_____
_____
_____
_____
_____
_____
_____
_____
_____

PROBLEM:

_____

_____

_____

STEP 1: Develop Your Understanding of the Problem

_____

_____

_____

_____

_____

_____

_____

_____

_____

_____

_____

_____

_____

_____

STEP 2: Develop a Hypothesis

_____

_____

_____

_____

_____

_____

STEP 3: Investigate/Gather Data (record sources if possible)

_____

_____

_____

_____

_____

_____

_____

_____

_____

_____

STEP 4: Analyze Your Results

_____
_____
_____
_____
_____
_____
_____
_____
_____
_____
_____
_____
_____
_____
_____
_____
_____
_____
_____

STEP 5: Apply Personal Preference (optional)

_____
_____
_____
_____
_____
_____

CONCLUSION:

_____
_____
_____
_____
_____
_____
_____
_____
_____
_____
_____

PROBLEM:

_____
_____
_____

STEP 1: Develop Your Understanding of the Problem

_____
_____
_____
_____
_____
_____
_____
_____
_____
_____
_____
_____
_____
_____

STEP 2: Develop a Hypothesis

_____
_____
_____
_____
_____
_____

STEP 3: Investigate/Gather Data (record sources if possible)

_____
_____
_____
_____
_____
_____
_____
_____
_____

STEP 4: Analyze Your Results

_____
_____
_____
_____
_____
_____
_____
_____
_____
_____
_____
_____
_____
_____
_____
_____
_____
_____
_____

STEP 5: Apply Personal Preference (optional)

_____
_____
_____
_____
_____
_____

CONCLUSION:

_____
_____
_____
_____
_____
_____
_____
_____
_____
_____
_____

PROBLEM:

_____
_____
_____

STEP 1: Develop Your Understanding of the Problem

_____
_____
_____
_____
_____
_____
_____
_____
_____
_____
_____
_____
_____

STEP 2: Develop a Hypothesis

_____
_____
_____
_____
_____
_____

STEP 3: Investigate/Gather Data (record sources if possible)

_____
_____
_____
_____
_____
_____
_____
_____
_____
_____

STEP 4: Analyze Your Results

_____
_____
_____
_____
_____
_____
_____
_____
_____
_____
_____
_____
_____
_____
_____
_____
_____
_____

STEP 5: Apply Personal Preference (optional)

_____
_____
_____
_____
_____
_____

CONCLUSION:

_____
_____
_____
_____
_____
_____
_____
_____
_____
_____
_____

PROBLEM:

_____

_____

_____

STEP 1: Develop Your Understanding of the Problem

_____

_____

_____

_____

_____

_____

_____

_____

_____

_____

_____

_____

_____

_____

STEP 2: Develop a Hypothesis

_____

_____

_____

_____

_____

_____

STEP 3: Investigate/Gather Data (record sources if possible)

_____

_____

_____

_____

_____

_____

_____

_____

_____

STEP 4: Analyze Your Results

_____
_____
_____
_____
_____
_____
_____
_____
_____
_____
_____
_____
_____
_____
_____
_____
_____
_____
_____

STEP 5: Apply Personal Preference (optional)

_____
_____
_____
_____
_____
_____

CONCLUSION:

_____
_____
_____
_____
_____
_____
_____
_____
_____
_____
_____

PROBLEM:

_____

_____

_____

STEP 1: Develop Your Understanding of the Problem

_____

_____

_____

_____

_____

_____

_____

_____

_____

_____

_____

_____

_____

_____

STEP 2: Develop a Hypothesis

_____

_____

_____

_____

_____

_____

STEP 3: Investigate/Gather Data (record sources if possible)

_____

_____

_____

_____

_____

_____

_____

_____

_____

_____

STEP 4: Analyze Your Results

_____
_____
_____
_____
_____
_____
_____
_____
_____
_____
_____
_____
_____
_____
_____
_____
_____
_____
_____

STEP 5: Apply Personal Preference (optional)

_____
_____
_____
_____
_____
_____

CONCLUSION:

_____
_____
_____
_____
_____
_____
_____
_____
_____
_____
_____
_____

PROBLEM:

_____
_____
_____

STEP 1: Develop Your Understanding of the Problem

_____
_____
_____
_____
_____
_____
_____
_____
_____
_____
_____
_____
_____
_____
_____

STEP 2: Develop a Hypothesis

_____
_____
_____
_____
_____
_____

STEP 3: Investigate/Gather Data (record sources if possible)

_____
_____
_____
_____
_____
_____
_____
_____
_____

STEP 4: Analyze Your Results

_____
_____
_____
_____
_____
_____
_____
_____
_____
_____
_____
_____
_____
_____
_____
_____
_____
_____
_____

STEP 5: Apply Personal Preference (optional)

_____
_____
_____
_____
_____
_____

CONCLUSION:

_____
_____
_____
_____
_____
_____
_____
_____
_____
_____

PROBLEM:

_____

_____

_____

STEP 1: Develop Your Understanding of the Problem

_____

_____

_____

_____

_____

_____

_____

_____

_____

_____

_____

_____

_____

_____

STEP 2: Develop a Hypothesis

_____

_____

_____

_____

_____

_____

STEP 3: Investigate/Gather Data (record sources if possible)

_____

_____

_____

_____

_____

_____

_____

_____

_____

_____

STEP 4: Analyze Your Results

_____
_____
_____
_____
_____
_____
_____
_____
_____
_____
_____
_____
_____
_____
_____
_____
_____
_____
_____

STEP 5: Apply Personal Preference (optional)

_____
_____
_____
_____
_____
_____

CONCLUSION:

_____
_____
_____
_____
_____
_____
_____
_____
_____
_____

PROBLEM:

_____
_____
_____

STEP 1: Develop Your Understanding of the Problem

_____
_____
_____
_____
_____
_____
_____
_____
_____
_____
_____
_____
_____
_____
_____
_____

STEP 2: Develop a Hypothesis

_____
_____
_____
_____
_____
_____

STEP 3: Investigate/Gather Data (record sources if possible)

_____
_____
_____
_____
_____
_____
_____
_____
_____
_____

STEP 4: Analyze Your Results

_____
_____
_____
_____
_____
_____
_____
_____
_____
_____
_____
_____
_____
_____
_____
_____
_____
_____
_____

STEP 5: Apply Personal Preference (optional)

_____
_____
_____
_____
_____
_____

CONCLUSION:

_____
_____
_____
_____
_____
_____
_____
_____
_____
_____
_____

PROBLEM:

_____

_____

_____

STEP 1: Develop Your Understanding of the Problem

_____

_____

_____

_____

_____

_____

_____

_____

_____

_____

_____

_____

_____

_____

_____

STEP 2: Develop a Hypothesis

_____

_____

_____

_____

_____

_____

_____

STEP 3: Investigate/Gather Data (record sources if possible)

_____

_____

_____

_____

_____

_____

_____

_____

_____

_____

_____

STEP 4: Analyze Your Results

_____
_____
_____
_____
_____
_____
_____
_____
_____
_____
_____
_____
_____
_____
_____
_____
_____
_____

STEP 5: Apply Personal Preference (optional)

_____
_____
_____
_____
_____
_____

CONCLUSION:

_____
_____
_____
_____
_____
_____
_____
_____
_____
_____
_____

PROBLEM:

_____

_____

_____

STEP 1: Develop Your Understanding of the Problem

_____

_____

_____

_____

_____

_____

_____

_____

_____

_____

_____

_____

_____

_____

_____

STEP 2: Develop a Hypothesis

_____

_____

_____

_____

_____

_____

STEP 3: Investigate/Gather Data (record sources if possible)

_____

_____

_____

_____

_____

_____

_____

_____

_____

_____

STEP 4: Analyze Your Results

_____
_____
_____
_____
_____
_____
_____
_____
_____
_____
_____
_____
_____
_____
_____
_____
_____
_____
_____

STEP 5: Apply Personal Preference (optional)

_____
_____
_____
_____
_____
_____

CONCLUSION:

_____
_____
_____
_____
_____
_____
_____
_____
_____
_____

PROBLEM:

_____
_____
_____

STEP 1: Develop Your Understanding of the Problem

_____
_____
_____
_____
_____
_____
_____
_____
_____
_____
_____
_____
_____
_____
_____

STEP 2: Develop a Hypothesis

_____
_____
_____
_____
_____
_____

STEP 3: Investigate/Gather Data (record sources if possible)

_____
_____
_____
_____
_____
_____
_____
_____
_____
_____

STEP 4: Analyze Your Results

_____
_____
_____
_____
_____
_____
_____
_____
_____
_____
_____
_____
_____
_____
_____
_____
_____
_____
_____

STEP 5: Apply Personal Preference (optional)

_____
_____
_____
_____
_____
_____

CONCLUSION:

_____
_____
_____
_____
_____
_____
_____
_____
_____
_____
_____

PROBLEM:

_____

_____

_____

STEP 1: Develop Your Understanding of the Problem

_____

_____

_____

_____

_____

_____

_____

_____

_____

_____

_____

_____

_____

STEP 2: Develop a Hypothesis

_____

_____

_____

_____

_____

_____

STEP 3: Investigate/Gather Data (record sources if possible)

_____

_____

_____

_____

_____

_____

_____

_____

_____

STEP 4: Analyze Your Results

_____
_____
_____
_____
_____
_____
_____
_____
_____
_____
_____
_____
_____
_____
_____
_____
_____
_____

STEP 5: Apply Personal Preference (optional)

_____
_____
_____
_____
_____
_____

CONCLUSION:

_____
_____
_____
_____
_____
_____
_____
_____
_____
_____
_____

PROBLEM:

_____
_____
_____

STEP 1: Develop Your Understanding of the Problem

_____
_____
_____
_____
_____
_____
_____
_____
_____
_____
_____
_____
_____
_____

STEP 2: Develop a Hypothesis

_____
_____
_____
_____
_____

STEP 3: Investigate/Gather Data (record sources if possible)

_____
_____
_____
_____
_____
_____
_____
_____
_____
_____

STEP 4: Analyze Your Results

_____
_____
_____
_____
_____
_____
_____
_____
_____
_____
_____
_____
_____
_____
_____
_____
_____
_____

STEP 5: Apply Personal Preference (optional)

_____
_____
_____
_____
_____
_____

CONCLUSION:

_____
_____
_____
_____
_____
_____
_____
_____
_____
_____
_____

PROBLEM:

_____
_____
_____

STEP 1: Develop Your Understanding of the Problem

_____
_____
_____
_____
_____
_____
_____
_____
_____
_____
_____
_____
_____
_____
_____

STEP 2: Develop a Hypothesis

_____
_____
_____
_____
_____
_____

STEP 3: Investigate/Gather Data (record sources if possible)

_____
_____
_____
_____
_____
_____
_____
_____
_____
_____

STEP 4: Analyze Your Results

_____
_____
_____
_____
_____
_____
_____
_____
_____
_____
_____
_____
_____
_____
_____
_____
_____
_____

STEP 5: Apply Personal Preference (optional)

_____
_____
_____
_____
_____
_____

CONCLUSION:

_____
_____
_____
_____
_____
_____
_____
_____
_____
_____

PROBLEM:

_____
_____
_____

STEP 1: Develop Your Understanding of the Problem

_____
_____
_____
_____
_____
_____
_____
_____
_____
_____
_____
_____
_____
_____

STEP 2: Develop a Hypothesis

_____
_____
_____
_____
_____

STEP 3: Investigate/Gather Data (record sources if possible)

_____
_____
_____
_____
_____
_____
_____
_____
_____
_____

STEP 4: Analyze Your Results

_____
_____
_____
_____
_____
_____
_____
_____
_____
_____
_____
_____
_____
_____
_____
_____
_____
_____
_____
_____
_____

STEP 5: Apply Personal Preference (optional)

_____
_____
_____
_____
_____
_____

CONCLUSION:

_____
_____
_____
_____
_____
_____
_____
_____
_____
_____
_____

PROBLEM:

_____
_____
_____

STEP 1: Develop Your Understanding of the Problem

_____
_____
_____
_____
_____
_____
_____
_____
_____
_____
_____
_____
_____
_____
_____

STEP 2: Develop a Hypothesis

_____
_____
_____
_____
_____
_____

STEP 3: Investigate/Gather Data (record sources if possible)

_____
_____
_____
_____
_____
_____
_____
_____
_____
_____

STEP 4: Analyze Your Results

_____
_____
_____
_____
_____
_____
_____
_____
_____
_____
_____
_____
_____
_____
_____
_____
_____
_____
_____

STEP 5: Apply Personal Preference (optional)

_____
_____
_____
_____
_____
_____

CONCLUSION:

_____
_____
_____
_____
_____
_____
_____
_____
_____
_____

PROBLEM:

_____
_____
_____

STEP 1: Develop Your Understanding of the Problem

_____
_____
_____
_____
_____
_____
_____
_____
_____
_____
_____
_____
_____
_____
_____

STEP 2: Develop a Hypothesis

_____
_____
_____
_____
_____
_____

STEP 3: Investigate/Gather Data (record sources if possible)

_____
_____
_____
_____
_____
_____
_____
_____
_____
_____
_____

STEP 4: Analyze Your Results

_____

_____

_____

_____

_____

_____

_____

_____

_____

_____

_____

_____

_____

_____

_____

_____

_____

_____

STEP 5: Apply Personal Preference (optional)

_____

_____

_____

_____

_____

_____

CONCLUSION:

_____

_____

_____

_____

_____

_____

_____

_____

_____

_____

PROBLEM:

_____

_____

_____

STEP 1: Develop Your Understanding of the Problem

_____

_____

_____

_____

_____

_____

_____

_____

_____

_____

_____

_____

_____

STEP 2: Develop a Hypothesis

_____

_____

_____

_____

_____

_____

STEP 3: Investigate/Gather Data (record sources if possible)

_____

_____

_____

_____

_____

_____

_____

_____

_____

STEP 4: Analyze Your Results

_____
_____
_____
_____
_____
_____
_____
_____
_____
_____
_____
_____
_____
_____
_____
_____
_____
_____

STEP 5: Apply Personal Preference (optional)

_____
_____
_____
_____
_____
_____

CONCLUSION:

_____
_____
_____
_____
_____
_____
_____
_____
_____
_____
_____

PROBLEM:

_____

_____

_____

STEP 1: Develop Your Understanding of the Problem

_____

_____

_____

_____

_____

_____

_____

_____

_____

_____

_____

_____

_____

STEP 2: Develop a Hypothesis

_____

_____

_____

_____

_____

_____

STEP 3: Investigate/Gather Data (record sources if possible)

_____

_____

_____

_____

_____

_____

_____

_____

_____

STEP 4: Analyze Your Results

_____
_____
_____
_____
_____
_____
_____
_____
_____
_____
_____
_____
_____
_____
_____
_____
_____
_____
_____

STEP 5: Apply Personal Preference (optional)

_____
_____
_____
_____
_____
_____

CONCLUSION:

_____
_____
_____
_____
_____
_____
_____
_____
_____
_____
_____

PROBLEM:

_____

_____

_____

STEP 1: Develop Your Understanding of the Problem

_____

_____

_____

_____

_____

_____

_____

_____

_____

_____

_____

_____

_____

_____

_____

STEP 2: Develop a Hypothesis

_____

_____

_____

_____

_____

_____

STEP 3: Investigate/Gather Data (record sources if possible)

_____

_____

_____

_____

_____

_____

_____

_____

_____

STEP 4: Analyze Your Results

_____
_____
_____
_____
_____
_____
_____
_____
_____
_____
_____
_____
_____
_____
_____
_____
_____
_____

STEP 5: Apply Personal Preference (optional)

_____
_____
_____
_____
_____
_____

CONCLUSION:

_____
_____
_____
_____
_____
_____
_____
_____
_____
_____
_____

PROBLEM:

_____
_____
_____

STEP 1: Develop Your Understanding of the Problem

_____
_____
_____
_____
_____
_____
_____
_____
_____
_____
_____
_____
_____
_____
_____

STEP 2: Develop a Hypothesis

_____
_____
_____
_____
_____
_____

STEP 3: Investigate/Gather Data (record sources if possible)

_____
_____
_____
_____
_____
_____
_____
_____
_____
_____

STEP 4: Analyze Your Results

_____

_____

_____

_____

_____

_____

_____

_____

_____

_____

_____

_____

_____

_____

_____

_____

_____

_____

STEP 5: Apply Personal Preference (optional)

_____

_____

_____

_____

_____

_____

CONCLUSION:

_____

_____

_____

_____

_____

_____

_____

_____

_____

_____

PROBLEM:

_____

_____

_____

STEP 1: Develop Your Understanding of the Problem

_____

_____

_____

_____

_____

_____

_____

_____

_____

_____

_____

_____

_____

STEP 2: Develop a Hypothesis

_____

_____

_____

_____

_____

STEP 3: Investigate/Gather Data (record sources if possible)

_____

_____

_____

_____

_____

_____

_____

_____

_____

STEP 4: Analyze Your Results

_____
_____
_____
_____
_____
_____
_____
_____
_____
_____
_____
_____
_____
_____
_____
_____
_____
_____
_____
_____

STEP 5: Apply Personal Preference (optional)

_____
_____
_____
_____
_____
_____

CONCLUSION:

_____
_____
_____
_____
_____
_____
_____
_____
_____
_____
_____

PROBLEM:

_____
_____
_____

STEP 1: Develop Your Understanding of the Problem

_____
_____
_____
_____
_____
_____
_____
_____
_____
_____
_____
_____
_____
_____

STEP 2: Develop a Hypothesis

_____
_____
_____
_____
_____
_____

STEP 3: Investigate/Gather Data (record sources if possible)

_____
_____
_____
_____
_____
_____
_____
_____
_____
_____
_____

STEP 4: Analyze Your Results

_____
_____
_____
_____
_____
_____
_____
_____
_____
_____
_____
_____
_____
_____
_____
_____
_____

STEP 5: Apply Personal Preference (optional)

_____
_____
_____
_____
_____
_____

CONCLUSION:

_____
_____
_____
_____
_____
_____
_____
_____
_____
_____
_____

PROBLEM:

_____
_____
_____

STEP 1: Develop Your Understanding of the Problem

_____
_____
_____
_____
_____
_____
_____
_____
_____
_____
_____
_____
_____
_____

STEP 2: Develop a Hypothesis

_____
_____
_____
_____
_____
_____

STEP 3: Investigate/Gather Data (record sources if possible)

_____
_____
_____
_____
_____
_____
_____
_____
_____
_____

STEP 4: Analyze Your Results

_____
_____
_____
_____
_____
_____
_____
_____
_____
_____
_____
_____
_____
_____
_____
_____
_____
_____
_____

STEP 5: Apply Personal Preference (optional)

_____
_____
_____
_____
_____
_____

CONCLUSION:

_____
_____
_____
_____
_____
_____
_____
_____
_____
_____
_____

PROBLEM:

_____
_____
_____

STEP 1: Develop Your Understanding of the Problem

_____
_____
_____
_____
_____
_____
_____
_____
_____
_____
_____
_____
_____
_____
_____

STEP 2: Develop a Hypothesis

_____
_____
_____
_____
_____
_____

STEP 3: Investigate/Gather Data (record sources if possible)

_____
_____
_____
_____
_____
_____
_____
_____
_____
_____
_____

STEP 4: Analyze Your Results

_____
_____
_____
_____
_____
_____
_____
_____
_____
_____
_____
_____
_____
_____
_____
_____
_____
_____
_____

STEP 5: Apply Personal Preference (optional)

_____
_____
_____
_____
_____
_____

CONCLUSION:

_____
_____
_____
_____
_____
_____
_____
_____
_____
_____
_____

PROBLEM:

_____

_____

_____

STEP 1: Develop Your Understanding of the Problem

_____

_____

_____

_____

_____

_____

_____

_____

_____

_____

_____

_____

_____

_____

_____

STEP 2: Develop a Hypothesis

_____

_____

_____

_____

_____

_____

STEP 3: Investigate/Gather Data (record sources if possible)

_____

_____

_____

_____

_____

_____

_____

_____

_____

_____

STEP 4: Analyze Your Results

_____
_____
_____
_____
_____
_____
_____
_____
_____
_____
_____
_____
_____
_____
_____
_____
_____
_____
_____

STEP 5: Apply Personal Preference (optional)

_____
_____
_____
_____
_____
_____

CONCLUSION:

_____
_____
_____
_____
_____
_____
_____
_____
_____
_____

PROBLEM:

_____
_____
_____

STEP 1: Develop Your Understanding of the Problem

_____
_____
_____
_____
_____
_____
_____
_____
_____
_____
_____
_____
_____
_____

STEP 2: Develop a Hypothesis

_____
_____
_____
_____
_____
_____

STEP 3: Investigate/Gather Data (record sources if possible)

_____
_____
_____
_____
_____
_____
_____
_____
_____
_____

STEP 4: Analyze Your Results

_____
_____
_____
_____
_____
_____
_____
_____
_____
_____
_____
_____
_____
_____
_____
_____
_____
_____

STEP 5: Apply Personal Preference (optional)

_____
_____
_____
_____
_____
_____

CONCLUSION:

_____
_____
_____
_____
_____
_____
_____
_____
_____
_____
_____

PROBLEM:

_____

_____

_____

STEP 1: Develop Your Understanding of the Problem

_____

_____

_____

_____

_____

_____

_____

_____

_____

_____

_____

_____

_____

_____

_____

_____

STEP 2: Develop a Hypothesis

_____

_____

_____

_____

_____

_____

STEP 3: Investigate/Gather Data (record sources if possible)

_____

_____

_____

_____

_____

_____

_____

_____

_____

_____

STEP 4: Analyze Your Results

_____
_____
_____
_____
_____
_____
_____
_____
_____
_____
_____
_____
_____
_____
_____
_____
_____
_____

STEP 5: Apply Personal Preference (optional)

_____
_____
_____
_____
_____
_____

CONCLUSION:

_____
_____
_____
_____
_____
_____
_____
_____
_____
_____

PROBLEM:

_____
_____
_____

STEP 1: Develop Your Understanding of the Problem

_____
_____
_____
_____
_____
_____
_____
_____
_____
_____
_____
_____
_____
_____

STEP 2: Develop a Hypothesis

_____
_____
_____
_____
_____
_____

STEP 3: Investigate/Gather Data (record sources if possible)

_____
_____
_____
_____
_____
_____
_____
_____
_____
_____

STEP 4: Analyze Your Results

_____
_____
_____
_____
_____
_____
_____
_____
_____
_____
_____
_____
_____
_____
_____
_____
_____
_____
_____

STEP 5: Apply Personal Preference (optional)

_____
_____
_____
_____
_____
_____

CONCLUSION:

_____
_____
_____
_____
_____
_____
_____
_____
_____
_____
_____

PROBLEM:

_____
_____
_____

STEP 1: Develop Your Understanding of the Problem

_____
_____
_____
_____
_____
_____
_____
_____
_____
_____
_____
_____
_____
_____

STEP 2: Develop a Hypothesis

_____
_____
_____
_____
_____
_____

STEP 3: Investigate/Gather Data (record sources if possible)

_____
_____
_____
_____
_____
_____
_____
_____
_____

STEP 4: Analyze Your Results

_____
_____
_____
_____
_____
_____
_____
_____
_____
_____
_____
_____
_____
_____
_____
_____
_____
_____

STEP 5: Apply Personal Preference (optional)

_____
_____
_____
_____
_____
_____

CONCLUSION:

_____
_____
_____
_____
_____
_____
_____
_____
_____
_____

PROBLEM:

_____
_____
_____

STEP 1: Develop Your Understanding of the Problem

_____
_____
_____
_____
_____
_____
_____
_____
_____
_____
_____
_____
_____
_____

STEP 2: Develop a Hypothesis

_____
_____
_____
_____
_____
_____

STEP 3: Investigate/Gather Data (record sources if possible)

_____
_____
_____
_____
_____
_____
_____
_____
_____
_____

STEP 4: Analyze Your Results

_____
_____
_____
_____
_____
_____
_____
_____
_____
_____
_____
_____
_____
_____
_____
_____
_____
_____

STEP 5: Apply Personal Preference (optional)

_____
_____
_____
_____
_____
_____

CONCLUSION:

_____
_____
_____
_____
_____
_____
_____
_____
_____
_____

PROBLEM:

_____

_____

_____

STEP 1: Develop Your Understanding of the Problem

_____

_____

_____

_____

_____

_____

_____

_____

_____

_____

_____

_____

_____

_____

STEP 2: Develop a Hypothesis

_____

_____

_____

_____

_____

_____

STEP 3: Investigate/Gather Data (record sources if possible)

_____

_____

_____

_____

_____

_____

_____

_____

_____

STEP 4: Analyze Your Results

_____
_____
_____
_____
_____
_____
_____
_____
_____
_____
_____
_____
_____
_____
_____
_____
_____
_____

STEP 5: Apply Personal Preference (optional)

_____
_____
_____
_____
_____
_____

CONCLUSION:

_____
_____
_____
_____
_____
_____
_____
_____
_____
_____

PROBLEM:

_____
_____
_____

STEP 1: Develop Your Understanding of the Problem

_____
_____
_____
_____
_____
_____
_____
_____
_____
_____
_____
_____
_____
_____

STEP 2: Develop a Hypothesis

_____
_____
_____
_____
_____

STEP 3: Investigate/Gather Data (record sources if possible)

_____
_____
_____
_____
_____
_____
_____
_____
_____

STEP 4: Analyze Your Results

_____
_____
_____
_____
_____
_____
_____
_____
_____
_____
_____
_____
_____
_____
_____
_____
_____
_____
_____

STEP 5: Apply Personal Preference (optional)

_____
_____
_____
_____
_____

CONCLUSION:

_____
_____
_____
_____
_____
_____
_____
_____
_____
_____

PROBLEM:

_____

_____

_____

STEP 1: Develop Your Understanding of the Problem

_____

_____

_____

_____

_____

_____

_____

_____

_____

_____

_____

_____

_____

_____

_____

_____

STEP 2: Develop a Hypothesis

_____

_____

_____

_____

_____

_____

STEP 3: Investigate/Gather Data (record sources if possible)

_____

_____

_____

_____

_____

_____

_____

_____

_____

_____

STEP 4: Analyze Your Results

_____

STEP 5: Apply Personal Preference (optional)

_____

CONCLUSION:

_____

PROBLEM:

_____
_____
_____

STEP 1: Develop Your Understanding of the Problem

_____
_____
_____
_____
_____
_____
_____
_____
_____
_____
_____
_____
_____
_____
_____
_____

STEP 2: Develop a Hypothesis

_____
_____
_____
_____
_____
_____

STEP 3: Investigate/Gather Data (record sources if possible)

_____
_____
_____
_____
_____
_____
_____
_____
_____
_____

STEP 4: Analyze Your Results

_____
_____
_____
_____
_____
_____
_____
_____
_____
_____
_____
_____
_____
_____
_____
_____
_____
_____
_____

STEP 5: Apply Personal Preference (optional)

_____
_____
_____
_____
_____
_____

CONCLUSION:

_____
_____
_____
_____
_____
_____
_____
_____
_____
_____
_____

PROBLEM:

_____

_____

_____

STEP 1: Develop Your Understanding of the Problem

_____

_____

_____

_____

_____

_____

_____

_____

_____

_____

_____

_____

_____

_____

STEP 2: Develop a Hypothesis

_____

_____

_____

_____

_____

_____

STEP 3: Investigate/Gather Data (record sources if possible)

_____

_____

_____

_____

_____

_____

_____

_____

_____

STEP 4: Analyze Your Results

_____
_____
_____
_____
_____
_____
_____
_____
_____
_____
_____
_____
_____
_____
_____
_____
_____
_____
_____

STEP 5: Apply Personal Preference (optional)

_____
_____
_____
_____
_____
_____

CONCLUSION:

_____
_____
_____
_____
_____
_____
_____
_____
_____
_____
_____

PROBLEM:

_____
_____
_____

STEP 1: Develop Your Understanding of the Problem

_____
_____
_____
_____
_____
_____
_____
_____
_____
_____
_____
_____
_____
_____

STEP 2: Develop a Hypothesis

_____
_____
_____
_____
_____
_____

STEP 3: Investigate/Gather Data (record sources if possible)

_____
_____
_____
_____
_____
_____
_____
_____
_____
_____

STEP 4: Analyze Your Results

_____
_____
_____
_____
_____
_____
_____
_____
_____
_____
_____
_____
_____
_____
_____
_____
_____
_____

STEP 5: Apply Personal Preference (optional)

_____
_____
_____
_____
_____
_____

CONCLUSION:

_____
_____
_____
_____
_____
_____
_____
_____
_____
_____
_____

PROBLEM:

_____
_____
_____

STEP 1: Develop Your Understanding of the Problem

_____
_____
_____
_____
_____
_____
_____
_____
_____
_____
_____
_____
_____
_____

STEP 2: Develop a Hypothesis

_____
_____
_____
_____
_____
_____

STEP 3: Investigate/Gather Data (record sources if possible)

_____
_____
_____
_____
_____
_____
_____
_____
_____
_____

STEP 4: Analyze Your Results

_____
_____
_____
_____
_____
_____
_____
_____
_____
_____
_____
_____
_____
_____
_____
_____
_____
_____

STEP 5: Apply Personal Preference (optional)

_____
_____
_____
_____
_____
_____

CONCLUSION:

_____
_____
_____
_____
_____
_____
_____
_____
_____
_____

PROBLEM:

_____
_____
_____

STEP 1: Develop Your Understanding of the Problem

_____
_____
_____
_____
_____
_____
_____
_____
_____
_____
_____
_____
_____
_____

STEP 2: Develop a Hypothesis

_____
_____
_____
_____
_____
_____

STEP 3: Investigate/Gather Data (record sources if possible)

_____
_____
_____
_____
_____
_____
_____
_____
_____
_____

STEP 4: Analyze Your Results

_____
_____
_____
_____
_____
_____
_____
_____
_____
_____
_____
_____
_____
_____
_____
_____
_____

STEP 5: Apply Personal Preference (optional)

_____
_____
_____
_____
_____

CONCLUSION:

_____
_____
_____
_____
_____
_____
_____
_____
_____
_____

PROBLEM:

_____

_____

_____

STEP 1: Develop Your Understanding of the Problem

_____

_____

_____

_____

_____

_____

_____

_____

_____

_____

_____

_____

_____

_____

STEP 2: Develop a Hypothesis

_____

_____

_____

_____

_____

_____

STEP 3: Investigate/Gather Data (record sources if possible)

_____

_____

_____

_____

_____

_____

_____

_____

_____

_____

STEP 4: Analyze Your Results

_____
_____
_____
_____
_____
_____
_____
_____
_____
_____
_____
_____
_____
_____
_____
_____
_____
_____

STEP 5: Apply Personal Preference (optional)

_____
_____
_____
_____
_____
_____

CONCLUSION:

_____
_____
_____
_____
_____
_____
_____
_____
_____
_____

PROBLEM:

_____
_____
_____

STEP 1: Develop Your Understanding of the Problem

_____
_____
_____
_____
_____
_____
_____
_____
_____
_____
_____
_____
_____
_____

STEP 2: Develop a Hypothesis

_____
_____
_____
_____
_____
_____

STEP 3: Investigate/Gather Data (record sources if possible)

_____
_____
_____
_____
_____
_____
_____
_____
_____

STEP 4: Analyze Your Results

_____
_____
_____
_____
_____
_____
_____
_____
_____
_____
_____
_____
_____
_____
_____
_____
_____
_____

STEP 5: Apply Personal Preference (optional)

_____
_____
_____
_____
_____
_____

CONCLUSION:

_____
_____
_____
_____
_____
_____
_____
_____
_____
_____
_____

PROBLEM:

_____

_____

_____

STEP 1: Develop Your Understanding of the Problem

_____

_____

_____

_____

_____

_____

_____

_____

_____

_____

_____

_____

_____

_____

_____

STEP 2: Develop a Hypothesis

_____

_____

_____

_____

_____

_____

STEP 3: Investigate/Gather Data (record sources if possible)

_____

_____

_____

_____

_____

_____

_____

_____

_____

_____

STEP 4: Analyze Your Results

_____
_____
_____
_____
_____
_____
_____
_____
_____
_____
_____
_____
_____
_____
_____
_____
_____
_____
_____
_____

STEP 5: Apply Personal Preference (optional)

_____
_____
_____
_____
_____
_____

CONCLUSION:

_____
_____
_____
_____
_____
_____
_____
_____
_____
_____
_____

PROBLEM:

_____
_____
_____

STEP 1: Develop Your Understanding of the Problem

_____
_____
_____
_____
_____
_____
_____
_____
_____
_____
_____
_____
_____
_____

STEP 2: Develop a Hypothesis

_____
_____
_____
_____
_____
_____

STEP 3: Investigate/Gather Data (record sources if possible)

_____
_____
_____
_____
_____
_____
_____
_____
_____
_____

STEP 4: Analyze Your Results

_____
_____
_____
_____
_____
_____
_____
_____
_____
_____
_____
_____
_____
_____
_____
_____
_____
_____

STEP 5: Apply Personal Preference (optional)

_____
_____
_____
_____
_____
_____

CONCLUSION:

_____
_____
_____
_____
_____
_____
_____
_____
_____
_____
_____
_____

Sources

Made in the USA
San Bernardino, CA
15 July 2020